Plant and Animal Fossils

by Libby Romero

Table of Contents

Tyrannosaurus rex was a huge **dinosaur**. This dinosaur lived millions of years ago. People found **fossils** of the dinosaur.

What are fossils? What types of fossils do people find? Read this book to learn about fossils.

Words to Know

amber

dinosaur

footprints

fossils

organisms

petrified

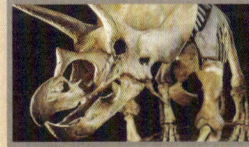
remains

sediments

tar

See the Glossary on page 22.

What Are Fossils?

Fossils are **remains** of plants and animals. The plants and animals lived long ago. The plants and animals were **organisms**.

▲ This fossil was a dinosaur.

Some fossils were dinosaur bones. Some fossils were **footprints**.

Some fossils were eggs.

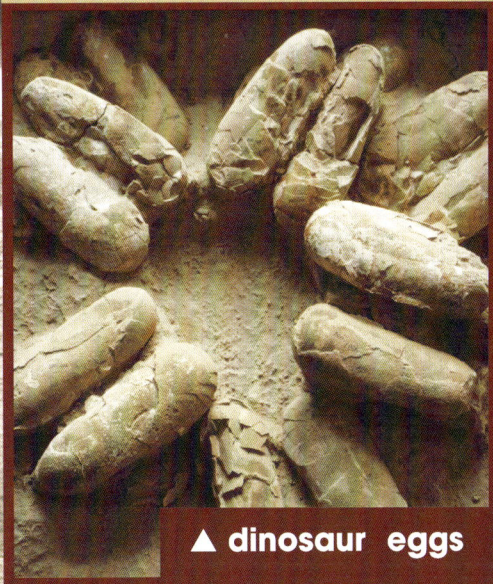

▲ dinosaur eggs

▲ These dinosaur footprints are fossils.

Some fossils formed from animals. Sand and clay buried the animals. Sand and clay are **sediments**.

▲ This fossil was buried in sand.

The soft parts of the animals rotted. The hard parts of the animals became minerals. The hard parts became fossils.

▲ These fossils were hard parts of animals.

Sometimes animals made footprints in sediment. The footprints became fossils.

▲ These fossils are dinosaur footprints.

Sometimes trees became fossils. The trees became **petrified**. The trees became stone. The stone trees are fossils.

▲ **These petrified trees are fossils.**

Solve This

Arizona has petrified trees. The trees are about six feet in diameter. Argentina has petrified trees. The trees are about ten feet in diameter. How much larger are the trees from Argentina?

Answer: about 4 feet larger in diameter

Where Do We Find Fossils?

Many fossils are in rocks.

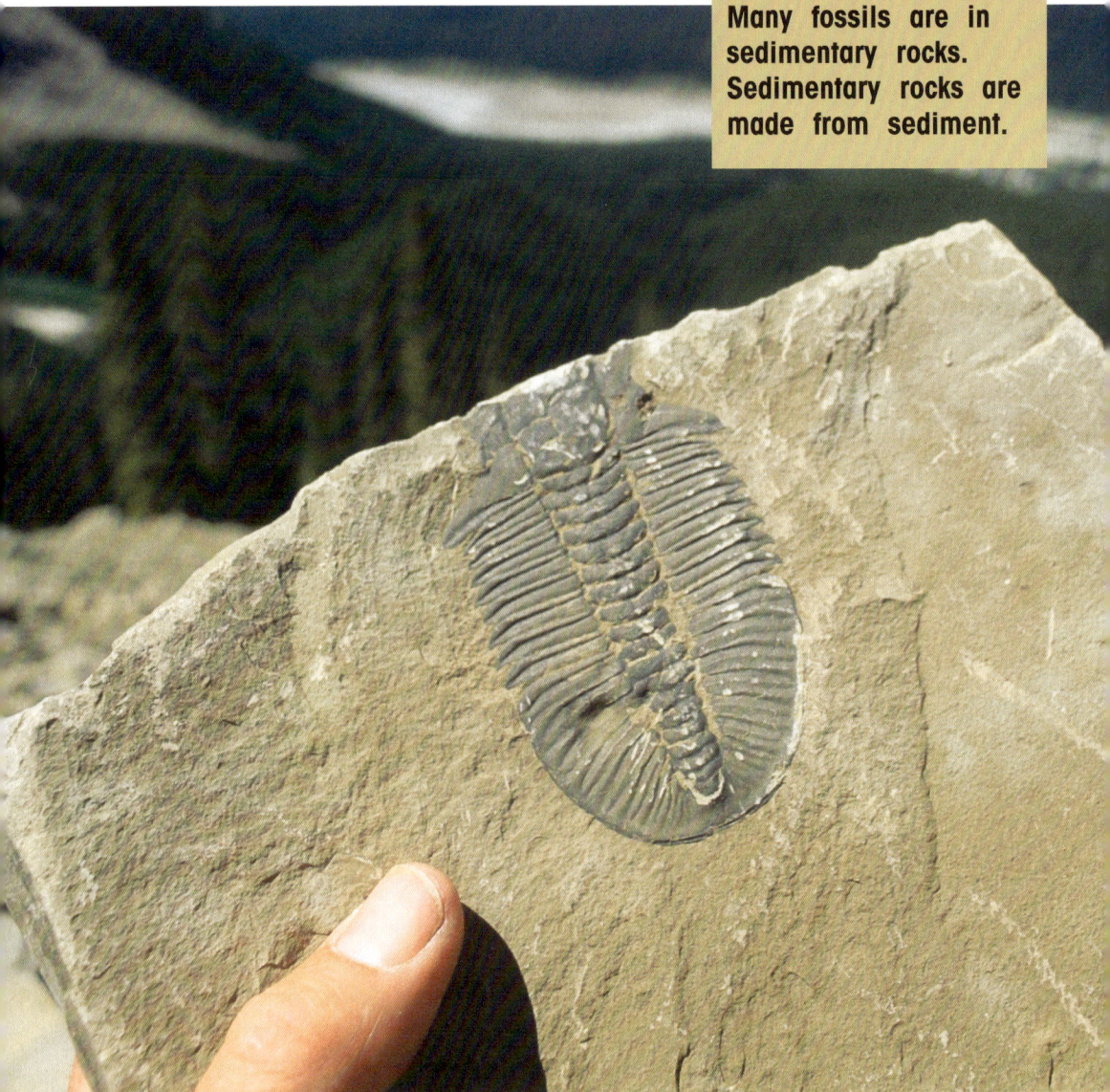

▲ This fossil is in a rock.

Fossils are in cliffs. Fossils are along rivers.

Some fossils are in **amber**. Amber is sap from trees. Insects were trapped in the sap. Then the sap became hard.

▲ This is the fossil of an insect.

Did You Know?

People use amber to make jewelry.

Some fossils are in **tar**. Tar is part of oil. Tar came to the surface of the ground. Animals were trapped in the tar.

▲ The La Brea tar pits are in Los Angeles. The tar pits are full of fossils. The fossils are of animals like these.

What Do We Learn From Fossils?

We learn about animals from fossils. We learn what animals looked like long ago. We learn about plants from fossils. We learn what plants looked like long ago.

▲ **This is the fossil of a horse. The horse lived 49 million years ago.**

14 **This is the fossil of a sea lily. ▶ The sea lily was a plant.**

We learn what animals ate long ago. We learn what animals ate meat. We learn what animals ate plants.

The Tyrannosaurus rex had sharp teeth. The Tyrannosaurus rex ate meat. ▶

▲ The Stegosaurus had dull teeth. The Stegosaurus ate plants.

We learn where animals and plants lived. The trilobite was a small ocean animal. Trilobite fossils are all over the world.

▲ **Trilobites lived in oceans.**

It's A Fact

Trilobites are extinct. There are no trilobites.

We learn how animals and plants changed. Saber toothed tigers lived long ago. Saber toothed tigers were a type of cat. Cats live on Earth today.

▲ **The saber toothed tiger had huge teeth.**

▲ **The cat does not have such large teeth.**

Try This

Make a Fossil
1. Flatten a large ball of clay.
2. Make the top of the clay smooth.
3. Press a shell or twig into the clay.

Some plants today look like plants from long ago.

We know about insects from fossils. We know about trees from fossils.

▼ **insect**

▲ **trees**

We know about dinosaurs from fossils. We know about leaves from fossils.

dinosaur ▼

▲ leaf

Summary

Fossils are remains of plants and animals. The plants and animals lived long ago. People find fossils in rocks. We learn about plants and animals from fossils.

Plant and Animal Fossils

What Are Fossils?

- remains of plants and animals
- bones
- footprints
- petrified trees

Where Do We Find Fossils?

- in rocks
- in cliffs
- along rivers
- in amber
- in tar

What Do We Learn From Fossils?

- about animals
- about plants
- what animals ate
- where animals and plants lived
- how animals and plants changed

Think About It

1. What are fossils?
2. How do fossils form?
3. What do we learn from fossils?

Glossary

amber sap from trees that became hard

*Insects get trapped in **amber**.*

dinosaur an ancient reptile that lived on land long ago

*People find **dinosaur** fossils.*

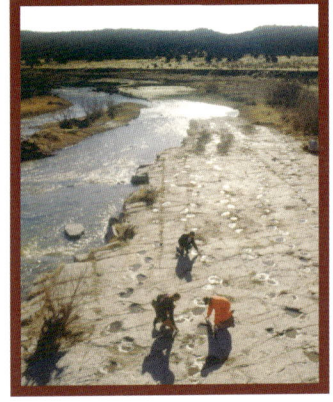

footprints marks made by the foot of a person or animal

*Some fossils are **footprints**.*

fossils remains of organisms

Fossils are remains of animals and plants.

organisms living plants or animals

*Animals and plants that lived long ago were **organisms**.*

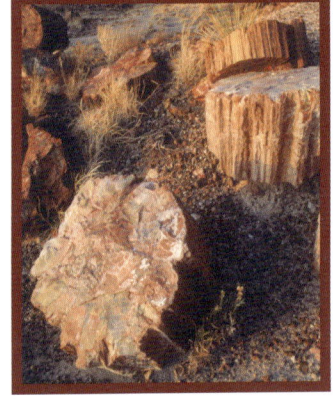

petrified turned to stone

Petrified trees are fossils.

remains what is left of something

Dinosaur bones are the remains of dinosaurs.

sediments sand and clay

Animals were buried in sediments.

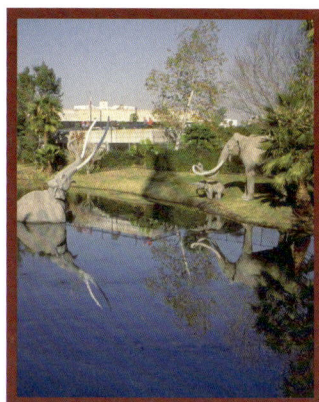

tar a thick, black liquid

Animals were trapped in tar.

Index